D1524687

LOOK!

Take a look around
the next time you are
outside. Where are
the most dangerous
areas for bicycle
riding? What could
you do to avoid
danger in
these places?

5

OUCH!

Accidents can really hurt. You could fall off your bike while riding too fast. You could run into something. You can get cuts, scrapes, and bruises. You could even break a bone. Accidents happen every day.

Doctors put broken arms and legs into casts to make sure they heal correctly.

Pretend you are riding a bike with a friend on a busy street. Should you ride side by side or one behind the other? It is much safer to ride one behind the other. You will be too far out in the road if you ride side by side.

7

YOU AND YOUR BICYCLE

Always keep your bicycle in good shape. Make sure nothing is loose or broken.

The chain should be tight. The tires should have plenty of air. The seat and handlebars should be just the right height. The brakes should always work.

Don't ride a bicycle if it has loose or broken parts. It could cause you to have an accident.

Ask an adult to show
you how to keep your
bicycle in top shape.
You might not be
able to fix a bicycle,
but you should
know when there is
a problem. Always
check your bicycle
before you go
for a ride.

9

Be sure to wear **safety gear**. It protects your body during accidents. Always wear a helmet. It should fit just right. Make sure it isn't too loose or too tight. Elbow and knee pads are important, too.

Your clothes should not be too loose. And watch out for untied shoelaces! They can get caught in your bike chain.

Wearing a helmet when biking will help prevent a head injury if you have an accident.

RIDE SMART

You should always be **alert** when you ride. You need to watch what is happening around you.

   Do not listen to music on headphones. Do not use a cell phone. Avoid talking to friends when there are cars nearby. Never fool around or show off on your bike.

Make sure you are always paying attention when riding your bike. Accidents can happen very quickly.

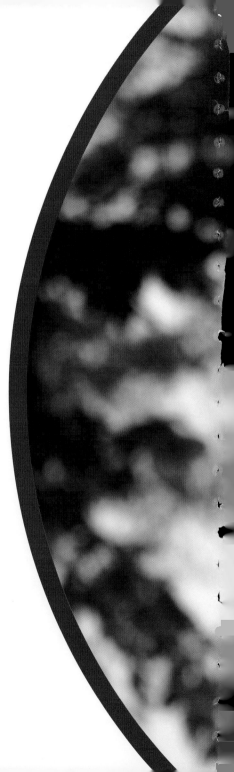

Try not to ride in the street. Always ride on the right-hand side if you have to go in the street. Ride in a straight line. Obey all road signs and lights.

Do not ride your bike through parking lots. They are filled with cars coming and going. The drivers might not see you.

Obey all signals and street signs. They are not just for cars.

Always use a **crosswalk** to cross the street. Get off your bicycle and walk it to the other side.

Be very careful at corners. You should stop before you get to a corner. You cannot see what is coming around the other side. Look carefully before you start riding again.

Using the crosswalk is the safest way to cross a street.

Do not ride on a road that has a lot of cracks or holes. Be extra careful on roads that are slippery from rain, snow, or ice. Avoid all roads that have heavy **traffic**.

Ride with your parents or friends if you can. Always bring a cell phone along if you have one. You can use it to call for help if something happens.

Don't ride on busy streets. Use roads with less traffic and only cross busy streets if you have to.

Make a map of your neighborhood. Then mark the best roads for bicycle riding. Use them as much as possible. Also, check to see if there are any bike paths near your home. There are no cars on bike paths!

19

The best time to ride your bike is during the day. You can see better in the daylight. People in cars can also see you better. Make sure your bicycle has **reflectors** and a light if you have to ride at night. You can also wear **reflective tape**.

Follow the rules and you will be safe on your bike!

Reflectors help other people see you and your bicycle more easily.

GLOSSARY

alert (uh-LERT) aware of what is happening around you

crosswalk (KROSS-wok) marked lines that show the right place to cross a street

dangerous (DAYN-jur-us) potentially harmful

exercise (ECK-ser-size) any activity that keeps your body healthy

reflective tape (re-FLEK-tiv TAYP) a type of tape that shines when light hits it

reflectors (ree-FLEK-terz) small pieces of plastic that shine when light hits them

safety gear (SAYF-tee GEER) pads and helmets people wear to protect their bodies

traffic (TRAF-ik) all of the vehicles on a road

SAFETY FIRST

Bicycle riding can be fun. It is very good **exercise**. You can spend time with your friends and family.

Riding a bike can also be **dangerous**. You can get hurt if you aren't careful. You should always follow safety rules.

Bike riding can be a lot of fun if you remember to stay safe!

CONTENTS

WHAT SHOULD I DO?

CHERRY LAKE Publishing

Published in the United States of America by Cherry Lake Publishing
Ann Arbor, Michigan
www.cherrylakepublishing.com

Content Adviser: Karen Sheehan, MD, MPH, Children's Memorial Hospital, Chicago, Illinois

Photo Credits: Cover and page 5, ©Monkey Business Images/Shutterstock, Inc.; page 7, ©Emin Ozkan/Dreamstime.com; page 9, ©Martinmark/Dreamstime.com; page 11, ©Jiri Hera/Shutterstock, Inc.; page 13, ©Ron Chapple Studios/Dreamstime.com; page 15, ©Jeff Martinez/Shutterstock, Inc.; page 17, ©Semen Lihodeev/Alamy; page 19, ©Huating/Dreamstime.com; page 21, ©donatas1205/Shutterstock, Inc.

LIBRARY OF CONGRESS CATALOGING-IN-PUBLICATION DATA
Mara, Wil.
 What should I do? on my bike/by Wil Mara.
   p. cm.—(Community connections)
 Includes bibliographical references and index.
 ISBN-13: 978-1-61080-055-6 (lib. bdg.)
 ISBN-10: 1-61080-055-9 (lib. bdg.)
 1. Bicycles—Safety measures—Juvenile literature. I. Title.
 GV1055.M36 2011
 796.60289—dc22   2011000127

Cherry Lake Publishing would like to acknowledge the work of The Partnership for 21st Century Skills. Please visit www.21stcenturyskills.org for more information.

Printed in the United States of America
Corporate Graphics Inc.
July 2011
CLFA09

ON MY BIKE

WHAT SHOULD I DO?

ON MY BIKE

BY WIL MARA

COMMUNITY · CONNECTIONS

?

FIND OUT MORE

BOOKS

Barraclough, Sue. *Bicycle Safety*. Chicago: Heinemann Library, 2008.

Donahue, Jill Urban, and Bob Masheris (illustrator). *Ride Right: Bicycle Safety*. Minneapolis: Picture Window Books, 2009.

Pancella, Peggy. *Bicycle Safety*. Chicago: Heinemann Library, 2005.

WEB SITES

KidsHealth—Bike Safety
kidshealth.org/kid/watch/out/bike_safety.html
Read more about staying safe when you ride your bike.

NHTSA—Kids and Bicycle Safety
www.nhtsa.gov/people/injury/pedbimot/bike/ kidsandbikesafetyweb/index.htm
Check out some bicycle safety tips from the U.S. National Highway Traffic Safety Administration.

INDEX

ABOUT THE AUTHOR

Wil Mara is the
award-winning
author of more than
120 books, many of
which are educational
titles for children.
More information
about his work can
be found at
www.wilmara.com.